MW00810256

Cider With Rosie

Laurie Lee

A stage adaptation by

James Roose-Evans

A SAMUEL FRENCH ACTING EDITION

FOUNDED 1830

SAMUELFRENCH.COM
SAMUELFRENCH-LONDON.CO.UK

Copyright © 1994 by James Roose-Evans and Laurie Lee
All Rights Reserved

CIDER WITH ROSIE is fully protected under the copyright laws of the United States of America, the British Commonwealth, including Canada, and all other countries of the Copyright Union. All rights, including professional and amateur stage productions, recitation, lecturing, public reading, motion picture, radio broadcasting, television and the rights of translation into foreign languages are strictly reserved.

ISBN 978-0-573-01735-3

www.SamuelFrench.com
www.SamuelFrench-London.co.uk

FOR PRODUCTION ENQUIRIES

UNITED STATES AND CANADA
Info@SamuelFrench.com
1-866-598-8449

UNITED KINGDOM AND EUROPE
Theatre@SamuelFrench-London.co.uk
020-7255-4302

Each title is subject to availability from Samuel French, depending upon country of performance. Please be aware that *CIDER WITH ROSIE* may not be licensed by Samuel French in your territory. Professional and amateur producers should contact the nearest Samuel French office or licensing partner to verify availability.

CAUTION: Professional and amateur producers are hereby warned that *CIDER WITH ROSIE* is subject to a licensing fee. Publication of this play does not imply availability for performance. Both amateurs and professionals considering a production are strongly advised to apply to Samuel French before starting rehearsals, advertising, or booking a theatre. A licensing fee must be paid whether the title is presented for charity or gain and whether or not admission is charged.

The professional rights in this play are controlled by Peters Fraser and Dunlop Ltd, Drury House, 34-43 Russell Street, London WC2B 5HA and Sheil Land Associates, 43 Doughty Street, London, WC1N 2LF.

No one shall make any changes in this title for the purpose of production. No part of this book may be reproduced, stored in a retrieval system, or transmitted in any form, by any means, now known or yet to be invented, including mechanical, electronic, photocopying, recording, videotaping, or otherwise, without the prior written permission of the publisher. No one shall upload this title, or part of this title, to any social media websites.

For all enquiries regarding motion picture, television, and other media rights, please contact Samuel French.

MUSIC USE NOTE

Licensees are solely responsible for obtaining formal written permission from copyright owners to use copyrighted music in the performance of this play and are strongly cautioned to do so. If no such permission is obtained by the licensee, then the licensee must use only original music that the licensee owns and controls. Licensees are solely responsible and liable for all music clearances and shall indemnify the copyright owners of the play(s) and their licensing agent, Samuel French, against any costs, expenses, losses and liabilities arising from the use of music by licensees. Please contact the appropriate music licensing authority in your territory for the rights to any incidental music.

IMPORTANT BILLING AND CREDIT REQUIREMENTS

If you have obtained performance rights to this title, please refer to your licensing agreement for important billing and credit requirements.

CHARACTERS

Narrator, Laurie Lee
Mother
Loll, the younger Laurie Lee
Marge
Mrs Davies
Mrs Pimbury
Rosie
Doth
Granny Wallon
Miss B
Baroness Von Hodenburg
Phyll
Granny Trill
Miss Wardell
Jo
Jack
Walt
Spadge
Vicar
Squire
Vincent
Mr Davies
Uncle Sid
Tony

CIDER WITH ROSIE

The original production of James Roose-Evans' stage adaptation, which he also directed, opened at the King's Lynn Festival, in the presence of HRH Queen Elizabeth, the Queen Mother, in 1963, moved to the Hampstead Theatre, and transferred to the Garrick Theatre, where it was presented by Michael Codron.

In the 1963 Garrick Theatre production the part of the narrator was played by William Squire, the mother by Daphne Anderson, the young Laurie Lee by Hywel Jones and Douglas Milvain played the roles of Squire, Mr Davies, Vincent and Uncle Sid. There was a subsequent production at the Greenwich Theatre in 1984 with the following cast of characters:

Narrator, Laurie Lee	Christopher Timothy
Mother	Barbara Ewing
Loll, the younger Laurie Lee	Simon Butteris
Marge **Mrs Davies** **Mrs Pimbury** **Rosie**	Claire Williamson
Doth **Granny Wallon** **Miss B** **Baroness Von Hodenburg**	Sarah Crowden
Phyll **Granny Trill** **Miss Wardell** **Jo**	Diane Paris
Jack **Walt** **Spadge** **Vicar**	Jeremy Swift
Squire **Vincent** **Mr Davies** **Uncle Sid**	Douglas Milvain
Tony	Richard Pearce

Directed by James Roose-Evans
Designed by Bruno Santini
Coach for accents: Elizabeth Pursey
Lighting by Chic Reid
Original music by Michael Hurd

PRODUCTION NOTE

THE NARRATOR

Laurie Lee's book is a poet's evocation of childhood. It is not a naturalistic tale. The actor must employ all the vocal variety and skills of rhetoric of which he is capable, otherwise it will become monotonous. He must vary rhythms, find different pitches, tempos, stresses, pauses, tones of voice. Yet it must never become self conscious beautiful speaking. It is not a recital. So the actor has a double challenge. He has to make every moment his own, and convince us that he is Laurie Lee and these are his memories. Yet he is not telling the story as Laurie Lee would in a reading. He is also conveying to us the intensity and immediacy of a poet's vision, the excitement and urgency of such discoveries, and the sheer intoxication at times of finding exactly the right words to paint his impression. It is, therefore, an enormously demanding role. And a lonely one. He is a part of the action and yet he is not acting with anyone. He is outside the action, he is the observer, seeing his childhood self, and yet the actor must never become patronizing, aloof, olympian, or voyeuristic. It is a role that takes courage, for music in words is not currently fashionable.

He must go out on to that stage with great excitement, knowing he is about to embark on a journey, and learn how he became a poet, and grow in understanding of his mother and of what he owes her. Once on that stage he must *enjoy* every word, every phrase, every image, sharing with the audience, wanting to communicate with us, as well as with himself. It is a voyage of self discovery taken before an audience. It is both private and public.

In the private moments he will discover many vulnerabilities. In the public moments he will enioy the art of the storyteller as, for instance, in the story of Jones's goat. Such passages are bardic, folklore, and he must take his fences boldly.

SETTING

If possible the setting should be a steeply raked stage with a ramp at the back so that the actors can be seen ascending the other side of the 'hill'. For the 1984 Greenwich production, as with the original West End production, the designer Bruno Santini used a circular tilted disc, with tall screens of gauze, pivoting in either direction along the back, providing both a background and a series of entrances and exits.

The play is not naturalistic, so that the images created by the director and actors must have the intensity of a painting. These images should flow from one to the other, using a choreographic approach. Props must be used sparingly and painted to tone in with the colours of the set. Essential to the production are: a set of old-fashioned kitchen chairs, pine and stripped, with vertical rods in the back rest and, if possible, the legs slightly splayed. These chairs, as will be seen, play many roles and achieve their apotheosis in the harvesting scene when they become sheaves of corn as they are laid diagonally across the stage. There is also a length of wood, about seven feet long and three feet wide, which is both table top and bed. This rests on two portable U-shaped structures, which become the table legs or the supports for the bed. These U-shaped structures also serve as the bar in the village pub or, placed together, become the box from the auction. There is a large cloth for the picnic scene, either green, or speckled with golden and green colour. There is a small wagon which serves for the family at the start of the play, and later for the funeral of Granny, and finally for the funeral of Mrs Lee, as well as the hay wagon in the cornfield. A coster's barrow will serve, which has a front wheel, and two upright supports at the back.

COSTUMES
The actors wear period costume of the pre-1914 era, as though they wore cast-offs and hand-me-downs. The boys basically have corduroy or tweed trousers, heavy boots (but felt the soles for sound) shorts, and neckerchiefs, with jackets for formal occasions, plus overcoats, scarves, mittens, balaclavas, as needed. There is a minimum of costume change as actors change character: a shawl, some pince-nez, a bonnet, (though Granny Trill has time to smooth her hair down tightly to the skull). Simplicity of staging is the key note.

A note for the actors: there must be a uniformity about the Gloucestershire accent. The actors must learn the shape of each scene, as in a painting, and know how to hold a stillness without being in any way static or posed. In rehearsal the actors need to search for truth in each small scene, and discover all the vitality, noisiness, energy and closeness of such a family, and then learn how to shape this so that each scene is carefully orchestrated. Realism is sought for, but not naturalism. Indeed, for this 'bucolic ritual' (as Harold Hobson described it in the *Sunday Times*) to work, the actors can never throw away, or be casual, televisual in their acting. Every moment has to be acted with a physical and vocal and imaginative intensity and concentration. It is very easy for this play, because it does not have the usual narrative build, to fall apart, and become slack. The director's task with this play is comparable to that of a conductor and also a choreographer.

James Roose-Evans

Laurie Lee's mother inherited four children by her husband's first marriage (Marge, Doth, Phyll and Harold — the latter not depicted in this stage adaptation) and her children by him were Jack, Loll and Tony. There was also a daughter who died at the age of four. She always grieved over the loss of this daughter of her own.

Laurie was born in 1914 and grew up during a time of change, when the rural traditions of past centuries were being swept aside in the path of twentieth-century progress. The book of *Cider with Rosie* has sold over four million copies and become a modern classic both in the United Kingdom and in America.

Music

Music for the songs and incidental music in the original production was composed by Michael Hurd. Enquiries regarding the use of this music should be made to The Hire Department, Novello & Co Ltd, Newmarket Road, Bury St Edmunds, Suffolk, JP33 3YB

NOTE

Please note that all programmes distributed in connection with performances of *Cider with Rosie* and in all instances in which the title of the play appears for the purposes of advertising , publicising or otherwise exploiting the play and/or production the following credit must appear:

CIDER WITH ROSIE
by
LAURIE LEE

A stage adaptation by
JAMES ROOSE-EVANS

Another stage adaptation by James Roose-Evans
also published by Samuel French Ltd:

84 Charing Cross Road
(from the book by Helene Hanff)

ACT I

A circular area with bunches of dried or artificial flowers around it and tall screens of gauze along the back which provide both a background and a series of entrances and exits (see Production Note)

As the House Lights lower we hear singing off stage, Michael Hurd's setting for:

> "O the wild trees of home...
> I want to see you rise.
> I want your lips of wet roses
> Laid over my eyes ..."

Ideally this should be sung solo

As the Lights come up there is a burst of chatter and laughter and the family rush up the slope, with the actor playing Mr Davies, etc., pushing the cart which is piled with chairs. Some of the boys also carry chairs. Loll carries a battered teddy bear. Mother clutches her hat. They rush up and then pause, at the top of the "hill", looking down to the small cottage on the other side of the valley

Jack Is that it?
Phyll It's got a pump and apple trees.
Marge Syringa and strawberries.
Loll A treasure in the walls!
Doth Rooks in the chimney.
Jack Frogs in the cellar.
Tony Mushrooms on the ceiling.
Mother And all for three and sixpence a week!

Immediate action. One girl piles two chairs C and deposits Loll there as on a raft, or crouched behind it. They unload the cart and it is taken off. The girls and Mrs Lee, who loves flowers, gather up the bunches and put them into jugs and containers

Laurie, the Narrator, walks down through this to L

Laurie We came to the village in the summer of the last year of the First World War, to a scattering of some twenty to thirty houses in a narrow steep valley. Living down there was like living in a beanpod: our horizon of · woods was the limit of our world. But on that first day we were all lost. Chaos was come in cartloads of furniture and I crawled the kitchen floor through forests of upturned chair legs. Our mother, too, was distracted from duty, seduced by the rich wilderness of the garden so long abandoned. All day she trotted to and fro, pouring flowers into every pot and jug she could find on the kitchen floor. I sat there on a raft of muddles, gazing through the window which was full of the rising garden.

The Narrator pauses and all are still, caught up for a moment in the stillness of the moment, Mother's arms full of flowers, gazing out

(Sudden shift of tone; briskly) The domestic arrangement of the house was shaken many times like a snowstorm toy ...

Coinciding with this line all lift the six chairs and swirl slowly upstage, holding the chairs high, as in a snowstorm toy, and set up the six chairs, UR for Loll's bed: three for the back and three for the front. Loll and Mother get in and one of the girls covers them with the eiderdown cloth

... so that beds and chairs and ornaments swirled from room to room, pursued by the gusty energies of Mother and the girls. But always these things resettled within the pattern of the walls. Nothing escaped or changed and so it remained for twenty years.

All action is completed. Mother and Loll are asleep. Laurie lies back on the floor DL. He sees the scene in his mind's eye out front

I was still young enough then to be sleeping with my mother. We slept together in the first floor bedroom on a flock-filled mattress in a bed of brass rods and curtains. So, in the ample night and the thickness of her hair, I consumed my fattened sleep, drowsed and nuzzling in her warmth of flesh, blessed by her bed and safety.

My mother, freed from her noisy day, would sleep like a happy child, humped in her nightdress, breathing innocently and making soft drinking noises in the pillow. In her flights of dream she held me close, like a parachute on her back, or rolled and enclosed me with her great tired body so that I was snug as a mouse in a hayrick.

During the following a strong shaft of light streams down through the screens on to the bed, like the sun rising

They were deep and jealous, those wordless nights, as we curled and muttered together, like a secret I held through the working day which set me above all others. It was for me alone that the night came down, for me, the prince of darkness, when only I would know the huge helplessness of her sleep, her dead face, and blind bare arms.

Mother rises and, arms stretched, yawning, she exits

The Lights continue to come up, covering the whole stage

At dawn, when she rose and stumbled back into the kitchen, even then I was not wholly deserted, but rolled into the valley her sleep had left, lay deep in its smell of lavender, deep on my face to sleep again in the nest she had made my own.

Laurie moves towards the area of the bed and his younger self. On the next line Loll is waking, stretching. He crawls to the edge of the bed

And then, waking one morning in the white-washed bedroom, I opened my eyes and found them blind. Though I stretched them and stared where the room should be, nothing was visible but a glare of gold, flat on my throbbing eyelids.

A robin is heard singing

I groped for my body and found it there. I heard the singing of birds. Yet there was nothing at all to be seen of the world save this quivering yellow light.
Loll Am I dead? Am I in heaven? Our Marge! I can't see nothing!

Marge and Doth appear from either side. They drop part of the eiderdown over the front of the chairs. It is gold and yellow and rust like autumn leaves

Marge Just look at him! Pop and fetch a flannel, Doth! 'Is eyes've got stuck down again.
Laurie The cold edge of the flannel passed over my face, showered me with water, and I was back in the world.
Loll 'Oo did it?
Marge Nobody, silly. Your eyes got bunged up, that's all.
Loll I'll bung up your eyes too. That's what I'll do.
Marge 'Ark at 'im, Doth. Isn't he a boy?

Marge exits

Doth folds the eiderdown neatly like a sheet

Laurie I was awake. I could see. I was happy. The world outside was crimson
and on fire. I'd never seen it look like that before.
Loll Doth, what's happening to them trees?
Doth Nothing's happening.
Loll Yes, it is then. They're falling to bits.
Doth (*yawning*) It's only the leaves droppin' — we're in autumn now. The
leaves always drop in autumn.

Doth exits

Loll remains gazing. Laurie upright behind him. Music (M. Hurd)

Laurie Autumn? Was that where we were?
Loll Where the leaves always drop and there is always this smell.
Laurie I had imagined it continuous, something that lasted for ever, like the
sharing of my mother's bed, with no change, for ever, those wet flames of
woods burning on and on ...
Loll Like the bush of Moses.

*They hold this for a moment. The music stops. Swift change. Note: during the
above, both must see and smell the autumn, but Loll is experiencing it for the
first time, storing up images for the later poet, while Laurie is recalling this
first time, as so often throughout the play. Here we may stress that the
objective for the actor playing the part of the grown Laurie is that of a man
in search of his lost childhood and reliving, sometimes painfully, all his
memories. This search reaches its peak in the poem that ends Act I. The actor
must never be detached from the action, waiting for his speeches to come up,
but live every moment as it unfolds, so that his speeches well up from the
action of memory*

Laurie I was never recalled to my mother's bed again.

The end of an era

Marge enters

*Swift activity. The chairs are reformed by the girls into a line UR, their backs
to the audience, on a slight curve, ready for the first school sequence. One
chair is brought downstage for Loll to sit on. It is as though the girls were
clearing after breakfast. Doth has Loll's scarf in her apron pocket, Marge the
cap, while the potato is mimed*

And that morning, when breakfast was over, my sisters surrounded me ...

They do so

... wrapped me in scarves ...

Action

... tied up my bootlaces ...

Action

... thrust a cap on my head...

Action

... and stuffed a baked potato in my pocket ...

The chair is pulled away from under him and placed CL

Loll What's this?
Marge You're starting school today.
Loll I ain't. I'm stopping 'ome.
Doth Now come on, Loll. You're a big boy now.
Loll I ain't.
Marge You are.
Loll Boo-hoo ...
Doth Boys who don't go to school get put into boxes and turned into rabbits and get chopped up on Sundays.
Laurie They picked me up bodily ——

Action

—— kicking and bawling, and carried me up to the road.

The stage becomes a playground. One of the girls brings out a skipping rope. Fit the action to the words, as Loll appears UC, facing the children in the playground

The playground roared like a rodeo. The rabble closed in, plucked at my scarves, spun me round like a top, screwed my nose, and stole my potato.

Schoolbell. All rush to sit in chairs UR. Loll sits in the chair downstage as the school teacher comes down to him

I was rescued at last by the teacher who boxed a few ears, dried my face and led me off to the Infants.

On "infants" the children upstage quietly start chanting their tables, and the teacher makes Loll sit in the chair

Teacher What are you staring at? Go on. Do tell. You needn't be shy.
Loll You're wearing a wig.
Teacher I can assure you I'm not!
Loll You are — I seen it.
Teacher I can assure you I'm not. Now look very close. Is that really a wig?
Loll (*looking hard*) Yes!
Teacher Well, really! I can assure you that it's *not* a wig! And if only you could watch me getting dressed in the morning you'd know it wasn't one either!

Loll stares — hold briefly

Laurie I spent that first day picking holes in paper, then went home in a rage.

Loll picks up chair and joins the end of the row. The chanting swells. The bell rings. All rise and race out of school

   Phyll appears carrying a bucket

The family greet Loll DR

Doth What's the matter, Loll? Didn't he like it at school, then?
Loll (*sitting on the floor*) They never gave me the present!
Marge The present! What present?
Loll They said they'd give me a present.
Doth Well, now, I'm sure they didn't.
Loll They did! They said, "You're Laurie Lee, ain't you? Well, you just stay there for the present!" So I sat there all day but I never got it. I ain't going back there again!
Laurie But after a week I felt like a veteran and grew as ruthless as everybody else!

Schoolbell. Each actor takes a chair or two and spaces them across the stage in two lines, great noise: they sit and start chanting in unison with Crabby B conducting them with her ruler

Chorus Twice one are two, twice two are four, twice four are eight, twice eight are sixteen. Twelve inches one foot, three feet make a yard, fourteen pounds make a stone, eight stone make a hundredweight, twenty hundred-weight make a ton. One God is love, One Lord is King, One King is George, One George is Fifth!

Miss B Stop shuffling your feet, Laurie Lee! A-smirking at that miserable Betty! I will not have it. I'll not, I say. I repeat ...

Chorus (*under breath*) *I will not have it!*

Laurie sits in the empty chair of the downstage row, facing front, the rest are seated with their backs to the audience

Laurie Miss B, the Head Teacher, was a bunched and punitive little body whom the school had christened Crabby. She had sour yellow hair coiled in earphones, and the skin and voice of a turkey. We were all afraid of the gobbling Miss B.

Voice 1 She spies!
Voice 2 She pries!
Voice 3 She crouches!
Voice 4 She pounces!
Chorus *She's a terror!*
Laurie We were all afraid of the gobbling Miss B, except Spadge Hopkins.

Spadge steps out on cue when needed

Miss B comes into the classroom

The children stand

Miss B Good-morning, children!
Chorus Good-morning, teacher!
Miss B Our Father, Which art in Heaven ...
Chorus Hallowed be Thy Name, Thy kingdom come, Thy will be done on earth as it is in Heaven. Give us this day our daily bread and forgive us our trespasses as we forgive those who trespass against us. And lead us not into temptation but deliver us from evil. For Thine is the kingdom, the power and the glory ...
Spadge She'd better look out. 'Er, Crabby B. She'd better, that's all. I can tell you.

He steps out of line as though to exit

Chorus For ever and ever. Amen!
Spadge Sod it all!
Miss B And where are you going, young man, may I ask?
Spadge If it's any business of yours!

Miss B Sit down this instant! (*Screaming*) I won't have it, I repeat — I will
not have it!
Spadge Ta-ta then!

Miss B goes to stop him. He grips and lifts her on to her chair UC, *as though
putting her on top of the cupboard*

Miss B Come and help me, someone! Come and help me!
Laurie But nobody moved. We just watched. We saw Spadge lift her up and
place her on top of the cupboard, then walk out of the door and away.

Spadge exits

*There is a moment of silence and then the Chorus stamp on the floor in unison,
starting quietly and building, as they rise and advance, surrounding Miss B,
lifting her up, as they chant*

Chorus Z - Y - X and W - V, U - T - S and R - Q - P, O - N - M and L - K
- J, I - H - G and F - E - D and C - B - A- *Crabby!*

The Chorus exits with Miss B

Laurie Crabby B was replaced by a new Head Teacher, a certain Miss
Wardley from Birmingham. She was more sober than Miss Crabby, her
reins looser but stronger, and after the first hilarity of her arrival and
strangeness, we accepted her proper authority. Not that she approved very
much of me.

Bell

*The schoolchildren enter, marching smartly, and taking their places. They
settle at once to lessons, murmuring quietly. Miss Wardley enters and
moves in and out*

Miss Wardley Fat and lazy, Laurie Lee! That's what you are. Wake up, you
and your little red eyes!

Loll sniffs

Sniff-sniff-sniff! Go out into the road and have a good blow and don't come
back until you're clear!

Loll leaves the classroom area and sits DR *on the very edge of the stage, and
Laurie in his chair swings round to look out front, never looking at the actor*

playing Loll (this only creates a suggestion of patronizing voyeurism! The Narrator sees it all in his mind's eye out front). The quiet murmur of lessons in the background and Miss Wardley moving quietly about, keeping attentive watch

Loll Of course I don't really belong to that lot at all. I'm summat different to them. I'm a — I'm a — young king. Yes! Placed secretly here in order to mix with the commoners. (*He sniffs*) There is clearly a mystery about my birth. One day the secret will be told. One day, they'll see, a gold coach with footmen in uniform will turn up suddenly, just like that! outside our kitchen door, and our Mother will cry and they'll stand very solemn and respectful to our Marge and Doth and Phyll and Jack and Tone, and then I shall drive off to my palace. I shall eat bacon and eggs off my throne. Course I shall be generous. I won't throw my brothers in a dungeon. No. Instead I shall give them a banquet of cakes and jellies and — things! And all my sisters, our Marge, our Doth, our Phyll, they shall have princes and they shall live in a palace in ... (*His imagination runs out here: Where shall it be? Ah yes*) *Stroud!*

The children in the classroom rise swiftly and start singing the national anthem, conducted by Miss Wardley

Chorus (*singing*) God save our gracious King ...
Loll And when I am King, Miss Wardley shall curtsy!

He joins the rest in place, singing loudly, aggressively

Chorus (*singing*) Long to reign over us, God save our King!

All sit, including Laurie

Miss Wardley A little less beastly now, Laurie Lee? How about bringing a hankie tomorrow? I'm sure we'd all be grateful.
Walt Kerry 'Ere, Loll, let me have a look at your sums.
Loll Yes, Walt, of course, Walt. Here. Copy them out. They ain't hard. I done 'em all.
Walt Kerry Ain't you a good scholar! You and your Jack. I wish I were a good scholar like thee.

Bell. All race out into the playground. The boys are very boisterous. The girls start a skipping game

Girls (*singing*) This is the way you brush your hair, brush your hair, brush your hair, This is the way you brush your hair, early in the morning.

The boys tease and chase the girls. The boys run to stand in front of chairs as though peeing. The girls clamber up on to chairs and "peer over"

Girls I can see! (*Etc.*)

Walt whispers something to Loll

Girl 1 I 'eard you, Walt Kerry! I 'eard what you said.
Girl 2 You be careful, you boys! I'll tell our teacher!
Boys Tell-tale tit! Cut her tongue and slit, and every little puppy dog shall have a little bit.

Bell. They return to the classroom. En route:

Walt D'you hear what I said then? Did you 'ear then? Eh? I told 'em. They didn't half squeal. (*Etc.*)
Miss Wardley You're a grub, Walter Kerry. You have the wits of a hen. You're a great hulking lout of a loaf. You can just stay behind, the lot of you!
Chorus *Oh, Miss!*

Laurie rises and steps to one side

Laurie When lessons grew too tiresome we had our traditional ways of avoiding them ...
Child 1 Please, Miss, I got to stay 'ome tomorrow, to 'elp with the washing——
Child 2 —the pigs——
Child 3 Me dad's sick——
Child 4 Please, Miss, you never learned us that ——
Child 5 I 'ad me book stole, Miss. Carrie Burdock pinched it——
Child 6 Please, Miss, I got a gurt headache.
Laurie At other times we forged notes from our mother or claimed to be the relations of corpses at funerals.
Child 1 It's me auntie, Miss ...
Child 2 It's me cousin Wilf, Miss ...
Chorus (*very strong*) Can I go please? Miss, can I go?

Three beats and then each picks up a chair, including Laurie and, led by him, they begin to circle the stage chanting, lit from overhead so that they are in silhouette

(*Chanting*) Ashes, to ashes, Dust to dust, If God won't have thee, The Devil must!

They repeat this twice then everyone, except Laurie, exits

Laurie Many a lone coffin was followed to its grave by a straggle of long-faced children, pinched, solemn, raggedly dressed — all strangers to the astonished bereaved!

Laurie waits for start of "The Ash Grove" being sung off stage, then, taking his chair, he crosses to R

Except for the hours we spent in school, our waking life and our growing years were for the most part spent in the kitchen and until we were married or ran away, it was the common room we shared.

All screens are now closed

The children enter with chairs plus table top and two uprights, and set up the table C

Doth carries a large basket containing all the necessary props: wooden plates, spoons, etc. But no food is served, the meal being mimed. This scene is set up during the next speech. Loll, with violin (if the actor can play one) and Jack with an exercise book and pencil, and Tony under the table with his cotton reels. The centre panel is left open for Mother. The lighting is warm and suggestive of firelight and then, when lamp lit, of oil lamp burning. Darkness beyond

Doth exits

Here we lived and fed in a family fug, lived on each other like birds in a hole, elbowed our ways without spite, all talking at once, or crying out against each other but never, I think,

Loll starts scales to coincide with the next line

(*crossing behind the table, close to Jack and Loll, en route to* L) feeling over-crowded, being as separate as notes in a scale.

Tony So they came out of this big hole, see, and the big chap said, "we'll kill 'em," see, and the pirates were waiting up 'ere, and they had this gurt cannon and they went bang fire and the big chap fell down wheee and rolled back into the 'ole and I said we got 'em and I run up the 'ill and seen this boat was comin' and I jumped on board whoosh crump and I said "now I'm captain see" and they said "fie" and I took me 'atchet 'ack 'ack and they all fell plop in the sea wallop and I sailed the boat round 'ere and round 'ere and up 'ere and round 'ere and down 'ere and up 'ere and round 'ere and down 'ere ...

Jack (*to Loll*) What's the name of the King then?
Loll Albert.
Jack No, it's not. It's George.
Loll That's what I said you, didn't I? George!
Jack No, you never. You don't know, you're feeble.
Loll Not so feeble as you be, any road!
Jack You're barmy. You got brains of a bed bug.
Loll Dadedadedadeda ...
Jack I said you're brainless. You can't even count.
Loll Turrelee, turrelee, didn't hear you!
Jack Yes, you did then, blockhead. Fat and lazy! Fat and lazy, Laurie ...
Loll Dadedadedadeda ... Can't hear!
Tony So they come out round 'ere and I chase 'em up 'ere and down 'ere and round 'ere ...

A crash of pots and pans and loud scream from Mother off

Mother enters at a rush with a tureen from C

Mother I'm all behind with the supper! If only I had a proper stove it wouldn't keep going out! *Loll!*
Loll Yes, our Mother?
Mother (*wiping her hands on apron*) See if Granny Trill's got a screw of tea, only ask her nicely, mind you!
Loll Ask our Jack, our Mother! I borrowed the bacon. It's blumming well his turn now!
Mother Loll!
Loll All right, our Mother.

Jack grins

Loll exits

Mother (*to Jack*) Poke around for the matches, dear boy. Damn me if I know where they got to.
Jack (*finding them in the large basket*) Here they are, Mother — in your work basket.
Mother Light the lamp, will you, and the candles. I can't see what I'm doing here in the dark.

Jack mimes lighting the lamp, which is an actual one on the table but must not be very high else it will mask faces at the table. The Lights come up

Loll enters and sits at the table, sucking in his lips

Loll I'm old Granny Trill, a-eating her dinner.

Mother clouts him

Mother Now don't mock the poor poor soul — alone by herself all day. Did you get the tea? Right, then, you can warm the pot, Loll. And Jack, you clear a place for the girls. (*She sets out the plates*) Come on, Tone, time for supper. Poor Granny Trill. The poor lone creature! It's a sin and shame. *Not my magazines!* (*She rescues them from Jack*) You boys ought to pop up and pay her a visit tomorrow. You know how she dotes on you.

The girls enter through the centre panel which closes behind them

They shed coats and shawls. Great noise, excitement: bedlam. The following should overlap, noisily, great affection and physicality. Best to get the cast to improvise it once or twice

Doth Hello, our Mother.
Mother Yoo-hoo!
Marge Hello, boys.
Phyll We're home.
Mother Where've you been? You're late.
Marge Hello, Ma.
Loll Got anything for us?
Tony Marge, Marge, Marge.
Phyll Here's some liquorice.
Tony Hello, Phyll, Hello, Doth. Look at my game, it's pirates!
Mother Oh, come by the fire, you look half dead!

They take their places at the table, but leave the centre chair for Mother even though she isn't going to get to sit in it for a while

Phyll It was murder in Stroud. I fell down twice in the High Street — *and showed my stockings!* I'm sure I showed everything. It was terrible, Ma. And a horse went through Maypole's window. And old Mr Fowler couldn't get down hill and had to sit on his *bottom* and slide! It's freezing harder than ever now. We won't none of us be able to budge tomorrow!

Mother serves the girls who eat at once. Tony sits on the floor leaning against Phyll's lap, and she hands him his food. She serves Jack

Doth Dr Green came up the shop this morning. Wearing corduroy bloomers. Laugh!

Loll Look, Ma, look! Look, Marge, Doth, hey — look, I've drawn a church on fire! Look!
Jack Ma, I haven't eaten all day! (*He has already had one helping and Loll none*)

Mother pushes Loll's dish away and serves Jack a second helping. She is all of a fluster. One of the girls rescues Loll and sees he gets some

Mother Whatever would the gentry say if they could see this table? Real gentry would have a fit!
Jack (*with his mouth full*) Why, Ma?
Mother (*holding the tureen in her arms, with cloth wrapped round it, and stirring absent-mindedly*) Why? For dining they'd have every place just so, that's why. The silver and the napkins — they had to be arranged in order, a set for every dish. First of all the butler would bring in the soup ——

She makes as though to ladle, perhaps does serve one of the children. They have all heard these stories many times, except perhaps little Tony

Chorus Scoop-scoop!
Tony (*echoing*) Scoop-scoop!
Mother Then he'd serve the ladies first. There'd be silver trout next or fresh salmon richly sprinkled with herbs and sauces.
Chorus Flick-flick.

Tony echoes

Mother Then some woodcock perhaps, or a guinea-fowl. Oh, yes, *and* a joint as well. And a cold ham on the sideboard, too, if you wished. For the gentlemen only of course. The ladies never did more than peck at their food.
Jack Why not?
Mother Oh, it wasn't thought proper. Then Cook would send in some violet cakes and there'd be walnut and fruit in brandy. You'd have wine, of course, with every dish. Mind you, it was a long hard day we girls had of it then. You'd be up before dawn, laying twenty or thirty fires; then there was all the sweeping, scrubbing, dusting and polishing; running up and down all them stairs answering all those bells that would always start ringing just as you put your feet up for two minutes. Five pounds a year, that's what I used to earn. Still, there was a lot of fun as well below stairs, and plenty to eat. I'll never forget Miss Emily's betrothal. What a picture she was! We were allowed a peep from the stairs. A man came from Paris just to do her hair. Her dress had a thousand pearls. There were fiddlers in

black perched up in the gallery. The gentlemen all wore uniform. Then the
dances — the polka — the two-step — the schottische....

*One of the girls lifts a small concertina from the basket and starts to play a
polka*

Oh, dear! I was carried away. We were all of us on the top landing, listening.
I was wicked in those days, I know. I seized hold of the pantry boy ...

*She grabs Loll and starts to dance with him around the stage, and the others
start dancing also*

and said, "Come on, Tom!" and we danced up and down the passage. Then
the butler found us and boxed our ears. He was a terrible man, Mr Bee.
Phyll Hush!
Doth Hark!

An owl hoots

Mother Hush!

A female owl responds

Phyll What's that?
Laurie We heard then, far away, down the lane, the drag of metal on frosty
ground, an intermittent rattle of chains.

All are listening intently

Phyll It's *him*!
Marge He's broke out again! It's *him*!
Mother Bolt the door, Marge. Doth, turn out the lamp.

They do so

Hush, keep quiet.

*Laurie moves to stand at the centre of the group. Phyll is crouched under the
table, holding and protecting Tony, their faces clearly visible*

Laurie The chains rattled nearer and nearer. Up the lane, round the corner,
along the top of the bank, then with a drumming of feet he was here! Frantic,
the girls leaped up with curious cries,

Action

stumbled their way across the firelit kitchen and clawed the dark curtains
back.

At once a harsh moonlight is cast across the group as they gaze front

Proud in the night, the beast passed by, head crowned by royal horns, his
milky eyes split by strokes of moonlight, his great frame shaggy with hair,
he moved with stiff and stilted strides, swinging his silver beard, and from
the tangled strength of his thighs and shoulders trailed the heavy chains
he'd broken ...

Doth ⎫ (*together*) *Jones's goat!*
Marge ⎭

Laurie Two words that were almost worship. For this was not just a straying
animal but a beast of ancient dream, the moonlight walker of the village
roads, half captive, half rutting king. He was huge and hairy as a Shetland
horse and all men were afraid of him. Squire Jones in fact kept him chained
to a spike driven five feet into the ground. Yet when nights were bright with
moon or summer neither spike nor chains could hold him. Then he snorted
and reared, tore his chains from the ground and came trailing his lust
through the village. But he walked alone. He encountered no-one. He
passed through an empty village. Daughters and wives peeped from
darkened bedrooms, men waited in shadows with axes. Meanwhile,
reeking with power and white in the moon, he went his awesome way!

Doth Did you ever see a goat so big?

Loll That knocks you down and tramples you. I heard he knocked down Miss
Cohen.

Marge mimes relighting the lamp

Marge Just think of meeting him coming home *alone*!

Doth Whatever would you do?

Marge I'd have a fit. What would you do, Phyll? Phyll?

Laurie But Phyll didn't answer. She had run away and was having hysterics
in the pantry!

Chorus Phyll!

*She climbs out from under the table. Marge collects her sewing bits from the
basket, Doth her darning, and Mother her scrapbook and scissors. A cosy
firelit scene of after-supper tasks*

Marge Look, Doth, I got these bits for sixpence. I'm going to stitch them all
round the top here.

Doth Hmmm. Well. Tcch-tch. S'all right.
Phyll Charlie Revell cheeked his dad today. He called him a dafty, he——
Mother (*singing*) I've got scraps, I've got scraps, I've got scraps for my
scrapbook ... Look, girls, a beefeater! Isn't he killing?
Doth You know that boy from the dairy, Marge? The one they call Barnacle
Boots? Well, he asked me to go to Spots with him. I told him to run off
home!
Marge No, you never!
Doth I certainly did. I said I don't want to go to no pictures with butter
wallopers! You should have seen his face.

Phyll has her arms round the now sleepy-flushed Tony

Phyll Do you remember, Doth, when we went to Spots and they said
Children in Arms Not Allowed? And we walked little Tone right up the
steps and he wasn't even two!
Loll Harry Lazebury smells of chicken gar. I had to move me desk.
Doth Just hark who's talking, Dainty Dick!

Mother looks up from her scrapbook

Mother   How many miles to Babylon?
Marge   Three score miles and ten.
Mother   Can I get there by candlelight?
Jack   Yes, and back again.
Mother (*addressing this to the absorbed Loll*)
                  If your heels are nimble and light
                  You'll get there by candlelight.

*It's as much as to say: Don't worry, son, about their teasing. You'll get there,
don't you worry. He will recall this verse in the second act when the mystery
and magic of words strikes him for the first time and he is able to make these
words his own*

Marge (*dreamily*) What couldn't I do to a nice cream slice! Give me some
tart, Ma.
Mother Give you some tart? (*She starts singing to tune of "Only a Rose"*)
Give me some tart ...

*This fades in to all of them singing very quietly or perhaps humming "Only
a Rose" as Laurie speaks*

Laurie Mother struggled to keep us clothed and fed. There was never much
money, the few pounds that our absent father sent us, but it was her own

muddle-head that Mother was fighting. Also her outbursts of wayward extravagance which splendidly ignored our needs. The rent was only three and sixpence a week but we were often six months behind. There would be no meat at all from Monday to Saturday, then on Sunday a fabulous goose, no coal or new clothes for the whole of the winter, then she'd take us all to the theatre, Jack, with no boots, would be expensively photographed; a new bedroom would arrive, then we'd all be insured for thousands of pounds, and the policies would lapse in a month.

Marge Go on telling us about the gentry, Ma. Tell us about Gaveston Court!

Mother Well, it was an old house, you know, very rambling and dark. A bit primitive, too, in some ways. But they entertained a lot — not just gentry but all sorts, even black men too at times! The master had travelled all round the world and he was a very distinguished gentleman. You never quite knew what you were going to run into. It bothered us girls at times. Well, one winter's night they had this big house party and the place was packed right out. It was much too cold to use the outside privy, but there was one just along the passage. The staff wasn't supposed to use it, of course. But I thought, oh well, I'll take a chance. Well, I'd just got me hand on the privy door when suddenly it flew wide open. And there, large as life, stood an Indian prince, with a turban, and jewels in his *beard*! I felt awful, you know. I was only a girl — I wished the ground to swallow me up. I just bobbed him a curtsy and said, "Pardon, your Highness!" But he only smiled and then folded his hands and bowed low and said,"Please, Madame, to enter!" So I held up my head and went in and sat down just like that. I felt like a queen.

Possibly one of the children softly sings the anthem, just a snatch. But they are very still, caught up in her memories. All focus on Mother, even the girls sewing. You can tell they are absorbing every word, even if their eyes are on their work. But Loll, next to his mother, above all is storing everything up

Phyll Tell us about the time you went to Aldershot, Ma.

Phyll says this, knowing her mother is in a storytelling mood. So Phyll can say this while snapping a thread with her teeth. She is not asking for a story but rather prompting, supporting, encouraging her mother

Mother Oh, yes, that was the time I was working in a big red house at a place called Farnham, Surrey. On my Sundays off I used to go into Aldershot to visit my friend Amy Frost — Amy Hawkins that was, from Churchdown, you know — before she got married that is ...

She is in danger of going off at a tangent here, quick!

Phyll *Ma!*

The others as well?

Mother Yes, well! This particular Sunday I'd dressed up as usual, and I do
think I looked a picture. I'd my smart lace-up boots, striped blouse and
choker, a new bonnet, and crochet worked gloves. I got into Aldershot far
too early so I just walked about for a bit. We'd had rain in the night and the
streets were shining and I was standing quite alone on the pavement when,
suddenly, round the corner, without any warning, marched a full dressed
regiment of soldiery. I stood transfixed: all those men and just me. I didn't
know where to look. The officer in front — he had beautiful whiskers —
raised his sword and cried out——
Boys *(Tony a step behind)* — *eyes right!*
Mother Then, would you believe it, the drums started rolling, and the
bagpipes started to play, and all those wonderful lads as they went
swinging by snapped to attention and looked straight in my eyes. I stood
all alone in my Sunday dress, it quite took my breath away. All those drums
and pipes and that salute, just for me — I just cried. It was so exciting.
Doth I wish one soldier would look at me like that, let alone a regiment.
Loll When I'm king I'll command a parade of Grannies!
Marge All Ma's talking has made me thirsty. Fetch me a cup of tea, Doth,
there's a dear!

Doth picks up a cup and saucer from the basket

Mother No, not that one! That's my beautiful porcelain cup. Get one from
the scullery.

*Loll rises to get one then turns back and looks down as his mother gazes at
the porcelain cup*

Laurie Old china to Mother was gambling and illicit love all stirred up
together; the sensuality of touch and the ornament of a taste she was born
to but could never afford. She hunted old china for miles around, though
she hadn't the money to do so, haunted shops and sales with wistful
passion, and by wheedling guile and occasional freaks of chance carried
several fine pieces home. She would stroke them and dust them, smiling
to herself, and place them in different lights; or just stop and gaze at them,
broom in hand, and sigh and shake with pleasure. She couldn't keep any
of them long however. She just had time to look them up in books, absorb
their shapes and histories, then guilt and necessity sent her off to Chelten-
ham to sell them back to the dealers. Sometimes, but rarely, she made a

shilling or two profit. But usually her cry was, "Oh, dear, I *was* foolish! I should really have asked them double."

Mother looks up from a newspaper

Mother There's a big auction today. Why did nobody tell me?

The children look guilty. They have been trying to conceal it from her

At Bisley. Oh, it's a splendid old place. The Delacourt family, you know. Very cultivated they were — or she was at least. It would be a crime not to go.

The Narrator honks a hooter

Oh, damn and blast there's the bus!

Another honk. The actors lift the table top on to its side and rest it against the uprights. They place chairs inside, with one at front for the driver, thus it becomes the bus. The Narrator takes a cap from his pocket and becomes the Driver. During the following the basket of props is struck. Loll and Jack help their mother. The others board the bus

Where's my gloves? Where's my handbag? Damn and cuss, where's my shoes? You can't find a thing in this hole! Help me, you idiots! Don't just jangle and jarl — you'll all make me miss it, I know.

Honk

There it comes!

Honk

Laurie, run up and stop it. Tell 'em I won't be a minute.

Loll races round the stage to the Driver

Loll Just coming, she says. Got to find her shoes. Won't be a minute, she says.

He races back. The passengers shake their heads

Passenger 1 Mother Lee again!
Passenger 2 Lost her shoes again.

Passenger 3 Come on, put a jerk in it there!
Mother I'm coming — yoo-hoo! Just mislaid my gloves. Wait a second. I'm coming my dears. (*She hobbles down the hill, basket on arm, clutching hat to head*)
Laurie Puffing and smiling, hat crooked, scarf dangling, clutching her baskets and bags she'd come hobbling at last through the stinging nettles and climb hiccuping into her seat. Then she'd call out to us.
Mother I shall only be looking. I shan't buy, of course. I just want to see them. SPODE!

Count 1-2 for laugh, then honk from the Driver

Laurie That evening, just as we were about to have tea, we heard her calling as she came down the bank.
Mother Boys! Marge! Doth! I'm home. Come and see!

The family gather round Mother DL

Laurie Mud-stained and flushed and just a little shifty, she came hobbling through the gate.
Mother Oh, you *should* have been there. Such china and glass. I never saw anything like it. Dealers, dealers, all over the place, but I did 'em all in the eyes. Look, isn't it beautiful? I just had to get it ... and it only cost a few coppers ...
Laurie She pulled from her bag a bone cup and saucer, paper thin, exquisite and priceless ...
Mother Of course, I could get those bits riveted!
Jack Ma, there's two men coming down the path with a gurt big packing case!

They gather round the box peering in

Mother (*giggling*) Oh, dear, I'd quite forgotten. That went with the cup and saucer. I had to take it. It was all one lot. But I'm sure we'll find it helpful.
Doth A ballcock?
Marge A bundle of stair rods!
Phyll An aigrette?
Tony The head of a spade?
Loll A boxful of sheep's teeth!
Doth And a framed photograph of Leamington Baths?
Marge Oh, Ma, you really are the limit!

The lighting changes: cold, a suggestion of snow

Phyll (*shivering*) It's freezing again.
Tony (*with wonder*) It's *snowing!*
Mother It's old Mother Jenkins up there a-plucking geese. We'd best go in.

*Loll remains c, singing softly. The others back him and Jack and Tony set up
the bed, taking the two uprights and laying them on their side UL, with the
table top across so that it is about ten inches off the ground. Mother goes to
sit in the centre of the three chairs, picking up a book, and taking spectacles
out of her apron pocket*

Loll   The north wind doth blow
                             And we shall have snow
                             And what will the robin do then?
                                         Poor thing!
                             He'll sit in a barn,
                             And keep himself warm,
                             And hide his head under a wing.

*Jack and Tony are now lying on the bed. Doth and Marge lead Loll on a
semicircular move up to the bed*

Doth Come on, Loll. Time to go to bed. The boys went up long ago.
Marge Wake up, lamb. He's whacked to the wide. Let's try to carry him up.
Laurie Half waking, half carried, they get me upstairs. It's cold in the
    bedroom. There are no fires here. Shivering I sway while the girls undress
    me, giggling around my buttons. Away goes the candle downstairs, doors
    creak, and the kitchen door shuts. My bed half is cold, Jack hot as a bird.
    For a while I lie doubled. Teeth chattering, blowing, warming against him
    slowly.
Jack Keep your knees to yourself. Say, think of a number.
Loll (*in a trance*) Eleven hundred and two.
Jack *Now double it!*

*Mother sits by the fire in the kitchen, combing Marge's blonde hair, quietly
talking. Loll lies, eyes wide open, listening*

Mother When my gran died I left service and went to work for my grandad
    in the inn at Sheepscombe. That's where I learnt to frogmarch, and there
    were plenty who got it! Pugs Sollars, he was the biggest bully in
    Sheepscombe — cider used to send him mad. He'd pick up the tables and
    lay about him like an animal while the chaps hid behind the piano.
    "Nance!" they used to holler, "for the Lord's sake, save us!" I was the only
    one who could handle him. I spent several years there and then one day I

read in the local paper, "Widower, with children, seeks housekeeper". And that's how I met *your* father.

Laurie He left us when I was three. When he'd gone my Mother brought us to the village and waited. She waited for thirty years. The few years Mother spent with Father she fed on for the rest of her life.

Mother He was proud of me then. I could make him laugh. "Nance, you're a killer!" he would say. He admired me, too; he admired my looks; he really loved me, you know. "Come on, Nance," he'd say, "Take out your pins. Let your hair down. Let's see it shine!" He loved my hair. So I'd sit in the window and shake it over my shoulders, and he'd twist it and arrange it so that it caught the sun, and then he'd just sit and gaze and gaze ... Sometimes, when you children were all in bed, he'd clear all his books away and say, "Come and sing us a song". We'd go to the piano and I'd sit on his lap and he'd play with his arms around me ...

She sings softly

> My old father years ago,
> Had a maid who loved him so,
> But their story went awry.
> So they kissed and said goodbye.
> Then a nightingale above
> Sang a melody of love.
> Years went by and still it lingered,
> Haunting night and day.

The Lights fade on the boys in bed

During the following verse Tony and Jack unobtrusively roll away

Mother }
Girls }   Once again, once again, once again,
> Sing, oh, sing, nightingale,
> For the sound of your song lingers on
> When the joy and the laughter are gone.
> For your song through the nights and days
> Will be here in my heart always.

The women quietly hum the melody under the following

Laurie In trying to recapture the presence of my mother I am pulling at broken strings. The years run back through the pattern of her confusions. Her flowers and songs, her unshaken fidelities, her attempts at order, her relapses into squalor, her near madness, her crying for light, her almost

daily weeping for a dead child-daughter, her frisks and her gaieties, her fits
of screams, her hysterical rages, her justice towards each of us children ...
Nothing that I see now that has the edge of gold around it — the change of
a season, a jewelled bird in a bush, the eyes of orchids, water in the evening,
a thistle, a picture, a poem — but my pleasure pays some brief duty to her.
She tried me at times to the top of my bent. But I absorbed from birth, as
now I know, the whole earth through her jaunty spirit.

The girls and Mother exit

Behind the gauzed screens stars appear. Frosty moonlight. Owls

Loll sits up, wide awake

Walt appears, in overcoat, balaclava and mittens, and leaps on to the stage

Walt Hey, Loll, wanna know summat?
Loll What, Walt?
Walt Shan't tell ya! (*He whistles and cleans his ears*) Well, if you wanna
know, I may as well ... Jones's pond is bearing ... I bin a-sliding on it all
morning. Millions bin coming wi' orses an' traps an' skates an' things an'
all. Remember I told ya. An' I got there first!

Walt exits

Music (M. Hurd). Laurie is UL, *just behind Loll*

Laurie   O river green and still,
                    By frost and memory stayed,
                    Your dumb and stiffened glass divides
                    A shadow and a shade.

                    In air the shadow's face
                    My winter gaze lets fall
                    To see beneath the streams bright bars
                    That other shade in thrall.

Loll moves downstage looking up

                    A boy, time fixed in ice ...

Snow falls, just as little Loll gazes up

His cheeks with summer dyed,
His mouth a rose devouring rose,
His bird throat petrified.

Loll races forward and falls, plucking at the snow. Laurie is right behind him

Loll

O fabulous and lost,
More distant to me now
Than rock drawn mammoth, painted stag
Or tigers in the snow!

He mimes punching a ball of snow together, still on his knees. Because Loll is on his knees, about to throw his "snowball", his head uplifted, and Laurie standing directly behind, it is almost as though while Laurie sees, in memory, his childhood self, Loll cannot see him

Laurie

You stare into my face,
Dead as a thousand years,
Your sparrow tongue sealed in my mouth
Your world about my ears.

Loll throws his "snowball" in a wide arc into the audience and stands looking out across the moonlit pond, all senses alert. The music returns under the last verse

And till our shadows meet,
Till time burns through the ice,
Thus frozen shall we ever stay —
Locked in this paradise.

There is a slow fade to Black-out

CURTAIN

ACT II

All screens are closed, the black side to the audience. The CURTAIN *rises in darkness, with a crack and roll of thunder. Strobe for lightning effect*

Figures in nightshirts are glimpsed, some with brooms, buckets, cloths

Mother Get up! It's coming in! Get up, or we'll all be drowned! More brooms! Run, someone, in the name of goodness! Sweep harder, boys. Sweet saints above! It's up to the doorstep already.

Laurie walks down through this

Laurie What panic those middle night rousings were, those trumpet calls murdering sleep, with darkness, whirlwind and invisible rain, trees roaring, clouds bursting, thunder crashing, lightning crackling, floods rising, and our mother demented!

Mother Oh, saints above, God in heaven! I can't *think* what I've done to be so troubled and tried. And just when I got the house straight.

Thunder

Laurie Our predicament was such that we lived at Nature's mercy, for the cottage, stuck on its steep bank, stood directly in the path of the floods and there was only one small drain to swallow them.

Mother Neither saints nor angels would keep their patience, if they had such things to put up with.

Lightning

Laurie When this drain blocked up, as it did in an instant, the floods poured into our kitchen.

Mother My poor, poor children, my precious darlings, you could die in this filthy hole. No-one would care — not a bell-essed soul — *Look out* with that damn and cuss bucket!

Everyone exits, pivoting the screens around to the gold and yellow sides

Laurie It was not till much later that I reasoned things out. That our position on the hillside made it unlikely we should drown, that Mother's frenzies and scares belonged to something else altogether and that it was possible after all to sleep through rain in peace.

The Lights come up

Our house was shaped like a T, and we lived in the downstroke. The top stroke was divided separately among two old ladies, one's portion lying above the other's. Granny Trill and Granny Wallon were rival ancients and lived on each other's nerves and their perpetual enmity was like mice in the walls. In all their time as such close neighbours they never exchanged a word. They communicated instead by means of boots and brooms, jumping on floors, and knocking on ceilings. They referred to each other as Er-Down-Under! Er-Up-Atop!

Er-Down-Under was a tiny white shrew who came nibbling through her garden and who clawed squeaking with gossip at our kitchen window or sat sucking bread in the sun. She lived on cabbage, bread and potatoes — but she also made excellent wines; Granny Wallon's wines were famous in the village and she spent a large part of the year preparing them.

Granny Wallon, in large white mob cap, and carrying a large basket, covered with cloth, appears and circles the rostrum

At the beginning of April she would go off with her baskets and would work round the fields and hedges and every fine day till the end of summer would find her somewhere out in the valley.

We'd see her come hobbling home in the evening, bearing her cargoes of crushed flowers, while she had buckets of cowslips, dandelions, elder-blossom, crammed into every corner of the house.

Projected on to the circular disc is a white flower of many petals which begins to revolve and Granny Wallon stands in the centre of it. Across the screens colours slide and revolve like a Chagall painting on the move

What seasons fermented in Granny Wallon's kitchen, what summers were brought to the boil. Gleanings of days and a dozen pastures, strippings of lanes and hedges, she bore them home to her flag-tiled kitchen, sorted them each from each, built up her fires and loaded her pots, and added her sugar and yeast. The vats boiled daily in suds of sugar, revolving petals in throbbing water, while the air, aromatic, steamy, embalmed, distilled the hot dews and flowery soups, and the wine ran down the dripping walls.

Granny Wallon exits

Whatever the small indulgences with which Granny Wallon warmed up
her old life, Granny Trill had none of them.

The Lights change to suggest the green mottled light under the great beech

Granny Trill enters DL, *carrying a bucket which she upturns and sits on.
She carries also a small basket*

For Er-Up-Atop was as frugal as a sparrow and as simple in her ways as
a grub. Her cottage was just outside our gate and her tiny room as visible
as last year's bird's nest.

The three boys enter, collecting kindling

Jack You at home, Granny Trill?
Loll You in there, Gran?
Granny Trill Well, I'll be bound. That you varmints again?
Jack We come on a visit, Gran. We brought you some kindling.
Tony What you doing, Gran?
Trill Just biding still. Just biding still and combing me bits.
Tony You be going bald, Gran?
Trill I still got me bits.
Tony It's coming out.
Trill No, it ain't.
Jack Look at that dead stuff dropping out of yer comb.

During the following, the boys look through her basket

Trill That's healthy. It makes room for more. (*Jumping up*) Er-Down-
Under! I got more than 'er. 'Er's bald as a tater root! Wicked old lump! I'll
see 'er gone, 'er's failing, you mark my words.

The boys have found a pair of drawers

Get your hands from me drawers! Them's female things. (*She sits again
and puts on her spectacles*) Just hand me that almanac there and let's see
what us have got in store. "Tragic intelligence of a Disaster at Sea, in the
Region of the Antipoods." That's for June, poor creatures, with their
families and all. "A Party of Scientists will slip down a Crevice with
Certain Resultant Fatalities". Oh, dear. Oh, well, if they must poke around
them places. "A Murdered Cadaver will be Shockingly Uncovered in a

Western Industrial Town". There, what did I tell you! I knew that'd come.
I been expecting that. (*She skips through the pages*) "Crisis in Parliament
... House Struck by Fireball ... Riots ... Turkish Massacre. Famine ... War."
Ah, well, he foresees some monstrous doings. A terrible year it looks to be.
And he says we'll have hail on Tuesday. (*She puts the spectacles in her
apron pocket*)

The boys are at her snuff-box

(*Catching them*) You at me snuff again, you boys? I'll skin yer bottoms,
I will!

They sneeze violently, and roll about. She chuckles

That'll learn you, I reckon; you thieving mites. Here, give it to me, I'll shew
'ee.
Laurie Snuff was Granny Trill's one horrible vice. A fine brown dust coated
all her clothes and she had nostrils like badger holes.
Tony You a hundred yet, Granny?
Trill Nigh on, nigh on.
Loll Have you got a dad?
Trill Bless you, no. He died long since. He was killed by a tree over
Ashcombe. My dad, he was a woodcutter, see. When I was five me ma died
and I went to live with me dad in the woods. We used to sleep in a sort of
wig-wam made of pine branches. I used to weave baskets and sell them
round the villages. That went on till I was fifteen and a big girl. By that time
me dad didn't use to like me going round the villages on me own ...
Tony Why not, Gran?
Trill You wouldn't know it now, but in those days I was quite a beauty. And
whenever the timber men came, my dad always used to hide me under piles
of sacking. Then one morning, while I was washing up breakfast things
outside our tent, I heard a tree, that had just been felled, come whooshing
down with a great splintering roar, and at the same time I heard me dad yell
out. I ran at once. The tree had fallen the wrong way and skewered him to
the ground. He was lying face down underneath the tree. He couldn't see
me. "I'm going, Alice," he said. I tore at the earth with my hands and made
him a hollow so that I could lie beside him and hold him until he died. It
took all that day and the night. He never spoke again. Next morning, some
of the carters found us. They rolled away the tree and straightened his
limbs. Then I ran away up the Scrubs and hid. I hid for a week, near some
fox holes. There was nothing to eat or drink. In the end the Squire sent some
men to look for me. When they found me I didn't half fight. I fought! I
fought like I was a heathen savage. But in the end they got me down to the

Manor and gave me a *bath*. That was the first bath I ever had. It took six of them to get me soaped ... A year after that, I was sixteen, I married George Trill, the gardener. He were a good man too — he settled me. He was much like me dad, only a good bit slower — and a lot older than I of course.

Pause

Me dad planted that tree outside there. He were a young man then, of course. He set it afore he got married.

Laurie The great beech filled at least half the sky and shook shadows all over the house. It roots clutched the slope like a giant hand, holding the hill in place.

Trill I got to see to summat!

The boys watch her going into the woods

Laurie Abruptly she left us, gathered up her skirts, and trotted lightly to the wood. We saw her squatting among the undergrowth, bright eyed, like a small black partridge. Old age might compel her to live in a house but for comfort she still went to the woods.

Everyone exits

Then one day as Granny Trill was clambering out of her wood, she stumbled and broke her hip. She went to bed then for ever.

Trill, backlit, appears in one opening

Laurie lies midway on stage

Trill I knowed it was coming after that visitation. I saw it last week sitting at the foot of my bed. Some person in white. I dunno.

The Lights crossfade to Granny Wallon in an opening on the other side. Granny Trill exits

Wallon Did you hear him, missus? He been ascreeching around since midnight. He called three or four times. In them yews. Her's going. You mark my words.

The Lights come up, woodland feeling. Off stage we hear the village singing "Abide with Me"

*During the following, the coffin, drawn by the actor playing Vincent, etc.,
circles from upstage, then downstage and stops* L. *The Villagers enter still
singing "Abide with Me"*

Laurie And that day indeed Granny Trill died whose bones were too old to
mend. The little church ——

A bell starts to toll

—— was packed for her funeral, for the old lady had been a landmark.They
carried her coffin along the edge of the wood, and they drew it on a cart
through the village. Granny Wallon, dressed in a shower of jets, followed
at some distance behind. All went well until the lowering of the coffin.

Wallon screams, forces her way through to the cart and looks at the coffin

Wallon It's a lie! That baggage were younger 'n me! Ninety-five, she says!
Ain't more than ninety, and I gone on ninety-two! It's a crime you letting
her go to her Maker got up in such brazen lies. Dig up the old devil! Get
'er brass plate off! It's insulting the living church!

Granny Wallon is dragged off. The coffin goes, leaving the stage empty

Laurie Granny Wallon had triumphed, she had buried her rival; and now
there was nothing more to do. From then on she faded and diminished
daily, kept to her house and would not be seen. About two weeks later, of
no special disease, Granny Wallon gave up in her sleep. She was found on
her bed, dressed in bonnet and shawl, with her signalling broom in her
hand. Her open eyes were fixed on the ceiling in a listening stare of death.
There was nothing in fact to keep her alive, no cause, no bite, no fury. Er-
Down-Under had joined Er-Up-Atop, having lived closer than anyone
else.

The Lights change. Wind

Mrs Davies enters DL, *followed by Mrs Lee, Jack and Loll and Tony.* UR,
*in the darkness, unseen by the audience, Mr Davies enters carrying his own
chair and blanket. He sits, swathed in the blanket*

The Lights come up on the group DL

Winter, of course, was the worst time for the old ones. Then they curled up
like salted snails.

Mrs Davies Come on in, Mrs Lee.

Mother We just called to ask how Mr Davies is faring.

Mrs Davies Poorly, poorly. He's real bad, Mrs Lee, and you can't really wonder at that. He's had ammonia for years. His lungs is like sponges. He don't know it but we reckon he's sinking. Here, you boys, here's a handful of peas to chew on. It was like this, Mrs Lee. He took ill on Friday. I sent for me daughter Madge. We fetched him two doctors, Dr Wills and Dr Packer, but they fell out over the operation. Dr Wills, you see, don't believe in cutting, so he gave him a course of treatment. But Dr Packer, he got into a pet over that, being a rigid one for the knife. But Albert wouldn't be messed about. He said he'd no mind to be butchered. "Give me a bit of boiled bacon and let me bide," he said. I'm with him there, of course. It's true, you know, once you've been cut, you're never the same again. Would you like to see him? Come on up, then.

Wind. They cross diagonally and Lights crossfade. Mrs Davies goes to the right of Mr Davies, while Mrs Lee and the boys stop in a small group to his left

Mother I brought the boys to see you, Mr Davies.

Mr Davies Do you know, Mrs Lee, I was sitting here last night just counting all of them as have been took and from Farmer Lusty's up to the Memorial I reckoned were nigh on a hundred. Best fasten the shutters, missus, the old bugger seems to snatch them at weekends. When I'm gone, see I'm decent, missus. Wrap up me doings in a red silk handkerchief.

Black-out

They all exit

Laurie Soon after the First World War a violent event took place in the village which drew us together in a web of silence and cut us off for a while almost from the outside world. The crime occurred a few days before Christmas.

Violin music off. The Lights come up on the pub area

The Barmaid enters, with the bar counter. The Fiddler and various Villagers, with tankards of beer, follow

The wind howls

The night was as cold as Cotswold cold can be with a wind coming straight from the Arctic. The men and youths were along at the pub drinking hot-pokered cider. Then the door blew open to a gust of wind.

A screen opens admitting a great shaft of light

*The silhouette of a man, Vincent, appears, his long shadow thrown across
the floor*

Vincent Hullo there, lads! Willy. Percy. Albert, isn't it? And, ah, it's
Cabbage Stump Charlie! Remember me, Vincent Barnes? Fisty Phil, how
are you, boy? Drinks all round! I only landed this morning at Bristol, from
an Auckland mutton boat. I hired a carriage but it broke down in the snow
so I had to finish the journey on foot. I'm on my way now to give the old
folks a Christmas surprise. I couldn't pass the old pub now, could I?
Laurie Everyone, save the youths, remembered this man. Years ago, he had
been packed off to one of the colonies, like many a poor boy before him.
Usually they went and were never heard from again. Now one of them had
returned like a gilded ghost.
Vincent I've done pretty well out there. Raised some cattle, made a heap
of money. It's easy enough if you have the guts and aren't stuck in the mud
like some I know. I mean, look at some of you! You've wasted your lives,
slogging for Squire for a miserable twelve bob a week, you live off
potatoes — not one of you has a sovereign to rub between you. You
youngsters will be just the same. All you ever see is muck, muck, and yet
more muck. And mebbe Stroud on a Saturday night. You see this? All
good money. See this gold watch? Why, it's solid gold. But that's nothing,
that's only a part of it. You should see my big farm I got in New Zealand—
horses — meat every day. And I never say "Sir" to no-one.
Laurie The old men kept silent, but drank their free drinks, while the youths
in the shadows just gazed at the man.

Action

Then, as he grew more drunk, they looked at one another and stole away
one by one.

*They stand in a huddled group in the dark UL, their backs to the audience. The
Barmaid strikes the counter as Vincent puts down his tankard*

When the public house closed, the New Zealander was the last to leave.
Vincent No, I don't want a lantern, thanks. I was born here, wasn't I? Good-
night — and Merry Christmas!

Snow begins to fall rapidly. Vincent goes up the hill singing

Laurie Warm with whisky and nearing home, he went singing up the hill.
There were those in their beds who heard his last song, pitched wailing
against the storm.

Wind stops

When he reached the stone cross the young men were waiting for him, a bunched group, heads down in the wind.

The snow stops

Men Well, Vincent?

The men surround him, action with words

Laurie They hit him in turn, beat him down to his knees, beat him bloodily down in the snow. Then they ripped off his coat, emptied his pockets, and left him.

Everyone but Vincent exits

He didn't stir from the place where he lay and in the morning he was found frozen to death.

The Lights crossfade to Laurie downstage

Vincent exits in the darkness upstage

The police came, of course, but discovered nothing. Their enquiries were met by stares. But the tale spread quickly from mouth to mouth, was deliberately spread among us, was given to every man and child, that we might learn each detail and hide it. The police left at last with the case unsolved, but neither we nor they forgot it.

A brilliant light comes up and all screens are reversed to their light side

Off stage we hear singing

Chorus (*off, singing*) "And did those feet in ancient times
                                    Walk upon England's mountains green,
                                    And was the Holy Lamb of God
                                    On England's pleasant pastures seen ..."
Laurie Summer, June summer! With the green back on earth and the whole world unlocked and seething! (*He takes off his jacket*)

The actors enter, each through a different opening

The Family race up, some carrying a giant green cloth which is unrolled down the slope. Tony carries a sketching book, one of the girls a basket, and Mother — as always — has flowers she has picked. She is in her best straw hat covered with flowers. Sound of cuckoos and pigeons. They gaze at the view. Some sprawl. Mother shades her eyes

Mother It's going to be hot later on, mark my words. Oh, what a picture it is. There's Painswick down there. Do you see? Green as green. And, look, those poppies, red as red? And there's Quedgley where I and my brothers were born. Funny how I were the only girl, and the ... Well, I got you daughters, of course, but I'd always wanted a daughter of my own, and she were only four! (*She breaks down*)

Phyll comforts her. The others watch anxiously

Phyll (*as a distraction*) Tell us about our uncles, Ma. Uncle Fred, the insurance man, and then Uncle Charlie, and ...
Mother Charlie the best woodsman in the Cotswolds ...
Laurie The new woods rising in Horsley now, in Sheepscombe, in Rendcombe, and Colne, my Uncle Charlie planted on thirty-five shillings a week ... His are these mansions of summer shade ...
Mother And then there was your Uncle Tom, oh he had a way with the girls, that is until he met Effie Mansell. Oh, she was a monster!
Chorus Why, Ma?
Mother Why? She were six feet tall, to begin with, and as strong as a cart horse. She no sooner decided that she wanted Uncle Tom than she knocked him off his bicycle and told him. The very next morning he ran away to Worcester and took a job as a tram conductor. He'd have better gone down the mines! She followed him and began to ride up and down all day on his tram, and what made it worse, he had to pay her fares! In the end his nerve broke, he muddled the change, and went to hide in a brick quarry. Well, Effie Mansell married the Inspector, and Uncle Tom settled down with your Aunt Minnie.
Jack I wish our Uncle Ray were here. Do you remember how he used to talk?
Loll (*with Canadian accent*) Waal, boys, I gotta be going.
Others Where you going, Uncle Ray?
Loll See a man 'bout a mule.
Others What for?
Loll Get my fingers pressed. Tongue starched. Back oiled.
Others You're fibbing.
Loll Just got to, boys. See you all in the oven. Scrub your elbows. Be good. So long!

All cheer the impersonation

Phyll Do you remember the time Uncle Ray came home on a bicycle?

Marge Yes, he'd been missing two days and he rode straight down the bank in the dark and crashed into the lavatory door! He was streaming with blood, and we had to drag him indoors and get him on the kitchen table, and then we took off his boots and *washed him*! Oh, what a state he was in, he smelled of whisky. And he sang and started to eat the soap and blew bubbles all over the kitchen. And then he had to go back to Canada, back to his railways. Trust him to blow himself up. He fell ninety feet down the Kicking Horse Pass and into a frozen lake.

Doth But Auntie Elsie travelled four thousand miles and she nursed him, brought him home, and married him!

Laurie lies on the ground but during the following he gets up and crosses to the other side

Laurie Our Uncle Sid was the best double-decker bus driver in Stroud, without doubt, even safer, more inspired when he drank. Everybody knew this, except the bus company. He began to get lectures, admonitions, stern warnings, and finally suspensions without pay. When this last happened, out of respect for our Aunt Alice, he always committed suicide. Indeed, he committed suicide more than any man I know. But always in the most reasonable manner. If he drowned himself, then the canal was dry. If he jumped down a well, so was that; and when he drank disinfectant there was always an antidote ready, clearly marked, to save everyone the trouble. He reasoned, quite rightly, that Aunt Alice's anger, on hearing of another suspension, would be swallowed by her larger anxiety on finding him again so near to death. And Auntie Alice never failed him in this and forgave him each time he recovered. The bus company were almost equally forgiving, they took him back again and again.

Loll Mam, do you remember the time when the bus company gave Uncle Sid the sack for good?

Tony Why?

Loll They found him asleep at the wheel — he were drunk! And that night, we were sitting by the fire when there was a knock at the door. It were Auntie Alice and the girls. They were all dressed in black. "He's done it this time," she said, "He's gone off to end it all. He's gone to Deadcombe Wood. He always told me he would!" And then she turned to our Mam and said, "Oh, Nance, Nance, he'll do himself in. Your boys, they just got to find him." So Jack and I put on our coats and we went up the valley, towards Deadcombe Wood. It were raining. We beat up and down through the wood, calling "Uncle, Uncle!" We were real scared. We didn't know what we might find. We were about to go home when suddenly we saw him. He were standing on tiptoe under an oak tree with his braces round his neck, looped to a branch. The elastic made him bob up and down! He were in a terrible temper. Do you know what he said?

Jack
Loll } *(together)* *"You've been a bloody long time!"*

Mother The sons of John Light, the five Light brothers ... We come from the oldest family in the world. We're down in the Book of Genesis. The Almighty said, "Let there be light!" — and *that* was long before Adam!

The sound of a pony and trap

Phyll Oh, Mam, there's a fine pony and trap!

They watch

Tony Look at all that harness.
Mother Do you know who it is? It's fisty Phil! That's what we used to call him. You know, I could have married if only I'd played my cards right.
Phyll Could you have, Mam? Really?
Mother Oh, yes, but I was choosy. Did I ever tell you how I shoved him into a brook over Sheepscombe way? To cool him off! 'Twere Sheepscombe where the blacksmith loved Miss Thwaite — she were a spinster and she used to make toffee in the back and sell it. She were *desperate* to marry, but the blacksmith be shy as blacksmiths be. Then, one day, she stole into the church and threw herself down on her knees. "Oh Lord," she prayed, "Please be mindful of me and send me a man to marry!" Now, by chance, the blacksmith were up in the belfry, mending the old church clock. Well, when he heard her pray, "Please send me a man!" he nearly fell off the roof, he were so excited! But he kept his head, tuned his voice to Jehovah's and boomed, "Will a blacksmith do?" "Any man's better than none, dear Lord!" cried Miss Thwaite gratefully. And so she married him and they used his forge for making their toffee. Ah, well, us had better be on our way else your Auntie Fan will think we're never coming. (*She starts off the poem*)
                    I remember, I remember
                    The house where I was born ...

She is gazing out Quedgley way. The children take up the poem as they strike camp. Mother remains gazing out front

Chorus
Mother }   The little window where the sun
                    Came peeping in at morn;

> The lilacs where the robin built,
> And where my brother set
> The laburnum on his birthday,
> The tree is living yet!

All, almost at the exit, turn and are still as Mother continues

Mother   I remember, I remember
                  The roses, red and white ...

Mother turns swiftly and exits. The others follow

Laurie The first choir outing we ever had was a jaunt in a farm wagon to Gloucester. Later, with the coming of the horse brake and charabanc, the whole village took part as well. One year the outing was to Weston-Super-Mare and we had saved up for months to be worthy of it.

Loll Come on, our Mother, they'll go without us!

Mother I just got to find me corsets. Poke about under the sideboard, dear boy, and see if you can find them.

Marge Oh, Ma, come on! Otherwise they'll go without us.

Mother Get the broom, Laurie, and give a good poke!

Doth Our Ma!

Mother Oh, run along, you're under my feet. I must wash myself first.

Laurie So we left her and scampered along to the Woolpack.

Each actor appears in turn carrying a chair

Mothers with big buckets stuffed with picnics, children with cocoa tin spades, fathers with bulging overcoats ——

Voice 1 —lined entirely with clinking bottles!

Laurie Little Miss Tulley, collecting the fares——

Voice 2 — and plucking at my nervous cheeks.

Laurie Mr Vick, the shopkeeper——

Voice 3 — carrying my keys in my shopping basket.

Laurie The two dressmakers——

Voice 4
Voice 5 } *(together)*   — in unclaimed gowns!

Laurie Lily Nelson, a fugitive from her brother, whispering ...

Voice 6 You mustn't tell Arnold, he'd kill me!

Laurie The squire's old gardener had brought a basket of pigeons——

Voice 7 —which I'm going to release from the pier!

Laurie And the postman, having nobody to deliver his letters to——

Voice 8 —has dumped the lot and is coming along too!

Laurie The last to turn up was the gravedigger ...
All What you got in that sack there, Sexton?

All look up at the sky

Voice 1 Don't look too good, do it?
Voice 2 Can't say it do.
Voice 3 Bloody black over Stroud.
Voice 4 Might clear though.

All shake their heads dubiously

Laurie The vicar arrived to see us off, his pyjamas peeping out from his raincoat.
Vicar There's a very nice church near the Promenade ... I trust you will all spare a moment. Here's a shilling for each choirboy!
Laurie And he dodged back home to bed. Then the charabanc arrived and everyone clambered aboard.

The cast place their chairs, two by two, down the ramp, facing the audience. At the front is a single chair for the driver, Uncle Sid, who will mime drinking from a bottle with one hand, and steering with the other. General pandemonium

Voices Harry! Hey, Harry! Say, whatcher, Harry! Bit of all right, ain't it! Hey, Bert! 'Ow you doing, ole sparrow? Where's Walt? Hey, there, Walt! (*Etc.*)
Uncle Sid Is everyone present?
Passenger 1 Mrs Lee's not here.
Passenger 2 Mrs Lee again.
Passenger 3 Lost her shoes again.
Passenger 4 Put a jerk in it there!
Mother Yoo-hoo! Just coming, my dears!
Voices Come on, Mrs Lee, we near went without you!
Mother I just had to wash my scarf!

She takes her seat. All jolt as it starts. Loud cheers. The Narrator stands to one side of the charabanc

Voices Put her in top, Uncle Sid! (*Waving handkerchiefs, singing*) "One man went to mow, went to mow a meadow, one man and his dog, went to mow a meadow." (*Etc.*)
Laurie Mile after rattling mile we went, under the racing sky, flying neck-

ties and paper kites from the back. Mother pointed out landmarks and
lectured the sleepers on points of historical interest. Then a crawling boy
found the basket of pigeons and the coach exploded ...

*Loud screams, some produce white handkerchiefs and climb on chairs as
though trying to catch pigeons*

The weather cleared as we all drove into ...
Chorus *Weston-Super-MARE!*

*They leap out of the bus, each taking their own chair. They spread out, gazing
at the sea front*

Voice 1 Where's the sea then?
Voice 2 It's all mud!

They sniff

Voice 3 Bit niffy, ain't it?
Voice 4 Don't half pong.
Voice 5 Oh, look, there's donkeys!
Voice 6 And the pier. Do you see?
Voice 7 Hey, Jake, Steve. Let's go have a wet!
Voice 8 I'm beat after that, Mrs Jones, ain't you? There's a clean place down
by the grandstand.
Voice 9 Oh, I don't think much of this Weston tea, do you, Mrs Lee? It's made
from the drains, I reckon.
Laurie The squire's old gardener, having lost his pigeons, was trying to catch
gulls in a basket.

Action with the chair

And the gravedigger, who appeared to have brought his spade was out on
the mud digging holes.

Action

Then the tide came and we all went on the roundabout.

*By now they have reached positions on the perimeter of circle so that each
actor sits—male, female, in sequence—astride a chair, in a circle, all facing
the same direction. As the hurdy-gurdy music starts, and the flashing
coloured lights, so they alternately rise and fall, laughing and shouting out
to bystanders; the Narrator moves into the centre collecting the fares. It*

stops. We hear the sound of the tide coming in. Sunset

When the tide went out, evening fell, and we returned to the waiting charabanc.

The hooter honks, all pick up the chairs and resume charabanc positions. After the initial burst of excitement, all are drowsy. Only Mother is still awake and this time Loll is next to her, in her lap, half asleep. Quiet singing, led by Mother, accompanied by a mouth organ, of "Home on the Range"

We passed Stroud at last and climbed the valley road, whose every curve our bodies recognized, whose every slant we leaned to, though still half asleep, till we woke to the smell of our house. And the Outing was over!

Brief pause, then tinkly piano music, and all set up chairs for front row of entertainment

The winter's village treat was the Parochial Church Tea and Annual Entertainment.

Either screens are used to make the stage, or two portable uprights, pole across and curtain on rings. All take their seats, including the Narrator. Great excitement. The curtains part and the Squire appears, in his deer-stalker hat and pince-nez. He hesitates, sighs, then turns to go. Whistles and cheers. Agitated whispers from the Vicar who reminds him of his speech

Squire Bless me! The Parochial Church Tea! (*Pause*) Is with us again. (*Pause*) I suggest. (*Pause*) And Entertainment. (*Pause*) Another year. (*Pause*) Another year has come round. When I see you all gathered here. (*Pause*) Once more. When I see ... when I think ... and here you all are! When I see you here — as I'm sure you all are — once again ... It comes to me, friends ... how time ... how you ... how all of us here ... as it were ...

He is weeping. He gropes his way through curtains. Loud and vigorous applause. The Narrator in his seat turns to face the audience

Laurie Turn followed turn in variety and splendour. Mr Crosby, the organist, told jokes and stories as though his very life depended on them, trembling, sweating, never pausing for a laugh, and rolling his eyes at the wings for rescue. We loved him and wouldn't let him go, while he grew more and more hysterical, racing through monologues, gabbling songs about shrimps, skipping, hopping, and jumping up and down as though humouring a tribe of savages. Major Doveton came next with his Indian Banjo. He straddled

a chair and began wrestling with the keys, cursing us in English and Urdu.
Then all the strings broke and he snarled off the stage. He was followed by
a play in which Marjorie, as Cinderella, sat in a goose feathered dress in a
castle. While awaiting for the pumpkin to turn into a coach she sang, "All
Alone by the Telephone".

Loud cheerful applause. The Vicar appears through the curtains

Vicar What is the smallest room in the world?
All A *mushroom*!
Vicar And the largest, may I ask?
All Room for improvement!
Vicar *You* know it! And now I have pleasure in introducing Mrs Pimbury
with a song about the mushroom!

*The curtains part to reveal Mrs Pimbury. The Vicar holds a song sheet so that
the stage audience and real audience can join in the chorus*

Mrs Pimbury   When I awoke the other morning
                       As the sun did rise,
                       Saw before me something strange,
                       It made me rub my eyes.
                       It wasn't there the night before,
                       Whatever could it be?
                       It wasn't very large and yet
                       I knew it was for me. So —

Chorus   Grow, grow, grow, little mushroom,
Mrs Pimbury   Grow grow, grow.
                       I know somebody wants you,
                       So, so, so.
                       I'll come again tomorrow,
                       Just you wait and see,
                       And if you've grown much bigger
                       You will just suit me.

Vicar All together now!

All   Grow, grow, grow, little mushroom,
                       Grow, grow, grow.
                       I know somebody wants you
                       So, so, so.
                       I'll come again tomorrow,

> Just you wait and see,
> And if you've grown much bigger
> You will just suit me.

Loud applause, hysteria, etc.

Laurie After Mrs Pimbury came slapstick, rough stuff about babies, chaps dressed as women, broad Gloucester exchanges between yokels and toffs with the yokels coming off best. We ached with joy and kicked at chairs, but we knew the end was coming.

More applause. The Vicar appears through curtains

Vicar And now for our guest star of the evening, the Baroness von Hodenburg from Sheepscombe, whom we are very honoured to have with us. She is a poetess and the author of many booklets. I know you will all give her a warm welcome.

Applause

The Baroness appears in a long gown, with a long ostrich feather and band around her forehead. She is given to eurhythmics

Baroness I am going to sing you a little ditty I convected myself. Bose words und music, I may say, is mine — und zey refer to ziss pleasant valley.

> Elfin folk, come over the hill,
> Come and dance just where you will.
> Bring your pipes and bring your flutes,
> Bring your sweetly sounding notes.
>
> Come away, come away!
> Life is gay, life is gay!
>
> Elfin folk, wherever you be,
> Come and join the dance with me.
> Bring your lutes and bring your lyres,
> Bring your sweetly sounding choirs.
>
> Come away, come away
> Life is gay, life is gay!

Feet stampede. Cheers, whistles. All pick up chairs. Commotion

Vicar Oranges will be distributed at the gate!

All exit and pivot the screens to black. The Narrator is alone, but chairs are `
set up L, *in a slight curve like a hedge, for Loll's and Jo's scene*

Laurie The week before Christmas, when snow seemed to lie thickest, was
the moment for carol singing. Steadily we worked through the length of the
valley, going from house to house, visiting the lesser and greater gentry —
the farmers, the doctors, the merchants, the majors and other exalted
persons. It was freezing hard and blowing too; yet not for a moment did we
feel the cold. The snow blew into our faces, into our eyes and mouths. But
we did not care. The collecting box grew heavier, and the list of the names
in the book longer.

The screens have opened, revealing the vista beyond, and the stars glittering.
The children, muffled and wrapped, and carrying lanterns, appear up the
ramp, singing "Noël, noël, noël!". They advance in a tight frozen group

We approached the last house high up on the hill, the place of Joseph the
farmer. The last stretch of country to reach his farm was perhaps the most
difficult of all. In these rough bare lanes, open to all winds, sheep were
buried and wagons lost.

Carol singers (*singing*)
In the bleak midwinter
Frosty wind made moan.
Earth stood hard as iron,
Water like a stone.
Snow was falling,
Snow on snow,
Snow on snow,
In the bleak midwinter
Long ago.

Laurie (*speaking*)
The sky cleared and broad streams
of stars ran down over the valley
and away to Wales. Everything
was quiet; everywhere there was a
faint crackling silence of the winter night. And two thousand Christ-
mases became real to us then; the
houses, the places of paradise, had
all been visited.

The carol singers, humming, now move to UR, *where a strong shaft of golden*
light beams down, as though they were standing at an open barn door

The group covers the quick escape of Loll and Jo who need time to shed
coats etc.

Laurie The stars were bright to guide the Kings through the snow, and
across the farmyard we could hear the beasts in their stalls. We were given
roast apples and hot mince pies, in our nostrils were spices like myrrh, and

Act II

in our wooden box, as we headed back for the village, there were golden gifts for all.

The carol singers exit. Loll and Jo enter

The Lights come up. Birdsong

Loll Where are you going then, Jo?

She wanders along the upstage side of the "hedge". Loll follows

Jo Nowhere special.
Loll Oh ... Let's go down the bank then. Shall us? Eh? Down the bank. Like before. How about it, Jo?

She steps through a gap in the chairs and he follows

Loll What shall we do then, Jo?

She does not answer

What d'you say, Jo?
Jo I don't mind.
Loll Come on, you tell.
Jo No — you.
Loll (*breezily like the doctor*) Good-morning, Mrs Jenkins! What seems to be the trouble?

She lies on her back, staring up. He kneels, mimes unbuttoning her dress. Discovering her breasts

Laurie Without a blink or a word Jo lay down on the grass. Silent as she lay, my hands moved as silently, and even the birds stopped singing. Her body was pale and milk green on the grass, like a birch leaf lying in the water, slightly curved like a leaf and veined and glowing, lit faintly from within its flesh. This was not Jo now, but the revealed unknown, a labyrinth of naked stalks, stranger than flesh, smoother than candle skins, like something thrown down from the moon. Night and home seemed far away. We were caught in the rooted trees. Knees wet with dew I pondered in silence all that Jo's acquiescence taught me. A blackbird screamed into a bush ...
Loll Well, that will be all, Mrs Jenkins. I'll be back again tomorrow.

He gallops away on an imaginary horse. Slowly she mimes dressing and goes home

Laurie Of course they discovered us in the end. Sooner or later one was always caught out, but the thing was readily forgotten. Such early sex games were formal exercises, grave in character, their ritual rigidly patterned. Our village was clearly no pagan paradise, neither were we conscious of showing tolerance. It was just the way of it. We certainly committed our share of statutory crime. Manslaughter, arson, robbery, rape, cropped up regularly throughout the years. Quiet incest flourished where the roads were bad, some found their comfort in beasts, and there were the usual friendships between men and boys who walked through the fields like lovers. Drink, animality, and rustic boredom were responsible for most. The village neither approved nor disapproved. But neither did it complain to the authority. So when in due time I breathed the first faint musks of sex, my problem was not one of guilt or concealment but of simple revelation. That early exploration of Jo's spread body was a solitary studying of maps. The signs upon her showed the way I should go then she was folded up and put away.

The Lights change. The screens pivot to golden and greens

The young people are waiting in shafts of light

Very soon I caught up with other travellers all going in the same direction. They received me naturally, the boys and girls of my age, and together we entered the tricky wood.

All enter energetically, the cart first which is set DL, with a large flagon of cider inside. They sing "We Plough the Fields and Scatter" and lay the chairs diagonally across the stage, in lines, each at an angle, so that they resemble sheaves of corn

Everyone exits

Birdsong. The Lights change

Rosie is lying downstage of the wagon

The day Rosie Burdock decided to take me in hand was a motionless day of summer.

Loll enters at a run, leaps over the sheaves, sees a crow, picks a stone throws it at the crow. He discovers Rosie

Loll Get out of there!

Rosie (*grinning*) I got summat to show ya.
Loll You push off!
Rosie You thirsty?
Loll I ain't, so there.
Rosie You be. C'mon. (*She drags out the cider jar*) It's cider. You ain't to drink it though. Not much of it at any rate.

He lifts it to his mouth

Go on!

Freeze action

Laurie Never to be forgotten, that first long secret drink of golden fire, juice of those valleys and of that time, wine of wild orchards, of russet summer, of plump red apples and Rosie's burning cheeks. Never to be forgotten or tasted again. I put down the jar.

Action

I turned to look at Rosie.

Rosie lies back

She was yellow and dusty with buttercups, her hair was rich as a wild bee's nest and her eyes were full of stings.
Loll Rosie!

Their faces close, their lips touch, part, then they roll over on next line, and freeze in a long embrace, faces apart, gazing at each other, he on top of her, but back arching upwards from her

Laurie The wagon under which we lay went floating away like a barge, out over the valley where we rocked unseen, swinging on motionless tides.

They break, laughing. They chase to the wagon

Then she took off her boots and stuffed them with flowers. She did the same with mine.
Rosie I tell 'ee what, Loll.
Loll What's that then, Rosie?
Rosie I like you.

Loll jumps on the wagon

Loll How much do you like me?
Rosie I like thee a lot better than Walt and ...
Loll And?
Rosie I like thee a lot better than Ken, or Boney Harris ... and I like thee a
lot better than the curate!

Loll laughs

  Rosie vanishes

The Lights change to moonlight. Owl cries

Loll Rosie! Rosie! Rosie!
Laurie I found myself wandering home alone, wet through, and possessed
by miracles. I discovered extraordinary tricks of sight.
Loll I can make trees move and leap frog each other. I can turn bushes into
roaring trains. I can fall flat on my face without pain and lick up the stars
like acid drops.

On this, he has leaped over a sheaf of corn, and thrown himself on the ground

Laurie I felt magnificent, fateful, and for the first time in my life, invulnerable
to the perils of the night.

*Loll looks up at the stars and the moon, sensing the huge immensity of it all
yet sensing also that it is out there he belongs. He is at home in the universe
and the childhood verse takes on the resonance of a poem*

Loll (*crying out the first line like a challenge to the universe*)
                How many miles to Babylon?

Almost he hears the echo

                Three score miles and ten.
                Can I get there by candlelight?
                Yes, and *back again!*

An owl hoots

Sisters (*off, distantly; long drawn out syllables*) Laurie! Laurie! Laurie!

Loll exits

Laurie It was then that I began to make up poems, hour after unmarked hour; while sisters called me, suns rose and fell, and the poems I made, which were never remembered, were the first and last of that time. *I was never the same again.*

The Lights come up to full

The last days of my childhood were also the last days of the village.

The sound of dance music played on the piano

The girls were to marry. The squire was dead. Buses ran and the town was nearer.

Actors appear, dancing and twirling. During the following they pick up chairs and twirl off with them as though the chairs were partners. The cart is also removed

We began to shrug off the valley and look more to the world. Each week Miss Bagnall held her penny dances where girls' shapes grew more familiar. Time squared itself up, and the village shrank and distances crept nearer. The sun and moon which once rose from our hill rose from London now in the east.

The screens close

Mother appears UL, holding a posy of wild roses

So with the family gone, Mother lived as she wished, knowing she'd done what she could, happy to see us, content to be alone, sleeping, gardening, cutting out pictures, writing us letters about the birds, going for bus rides, visiting friends, reading Ruskin or the *Lives of the Saints.*

Then suddenly our absent father died. And with that, his death, which was also the death of hope, our Mother gave up her life. Their long separation had come to an end, and it was the coldness of that which killed her. She had raised his two families, faithfully and alone — had waited thirty-five years for his praise. And through all that time she had clung to one fantasy — that at last, in need, he might one day return to her. His death killed that promise, and also ended her reason.

Mother abruptly, harshly, throws the posy on the floor. Slowly, she turns and exits

She never mentioned him again, but spoke to shades, saw visions, and then she died.

Off stage the singing of "Abide with Me"

The coffin, draped in black, on the cart, appears UR, and follows a circular passage downstage and up and around, until UR. The mourners follow, Loll last, now in a suit. The Narrator follows him. As the coffin is passing upstage, Loll is about C, sees the flowers, stoops, picks them up, and begins to speak his poem. By the last verse, the Narrator is close behind him, the boy and man now one, the search ended

Loll (*coming in over the end of the hymn*)
My mother would grow roses with each hand,
drawing them forth from country frothing air.

Draw them, shape them, cut them from the thorn;
lay them like bleeding shells about the house.

And with my ears to the lips of those shell roses
I harked to their humming seas, secret as hives.

And with my lips to those same rose-shell ears,
I spoke my crimson words, my stinging brain.

With lips, ears, eyes and every finger's nerve,
I moved, moth throbbing, round each creviced fire.

Laurie   As I do now, lost Mother, country gone,
groping my grief around your moss-rose heart.

Slow fade to Black-out. Loll and Laurie are C. The others, all in black, stand behind the coffin on the cart, UR, their backs away from Loll

CURTAIN

FURNITURE AND PROPERTY LIST

ACT I

On stage: Dried, or artificial, flowers
Hooter for **Narrator**
Shopping basket for **Mother**
Packing case
Book

Off stage: Cart. *On it*: part set of 6 kitchen chairs; length of wood (approximately seven feet long and three feet wide); 2 portable U-shaped structures; jugs; containers; gold, yellow and rust coloured eiderdown cloth (**Mr Davies**)
Remaining kitchen chairs from the set (**Boys**)
Skipping rope (**Girl**)
Bucket (**Phyll**)
Large basket containing wooden plates, spoons, box of matches, magazines, small concertina, sewing, darning, scrapbook and scissors, newspaper, cup and saucer, shopping basket (**Doth**)
Violin (**Loll**)
Exercise book, pencil (**Jack**)
Cotton reels (**Tony**)
Tureen, ladle (**Mother**)
Snow (**Stage Management**)

Personal: **Loll**: battered teddy bear
Doth: scarf for **Loll** in apron pocket
Marge: cap for **Loll**
Miss B: ruler
Phyll: bag of liquorice
Narrator: cap in pocket
Mother: spectacles and comb in apron pocket

ACT II

On stage: Six kitchen chairs

Off stage: Brooms, buckets, cloths (**Cast**)
              Large basket covered with cloth (**Granny Wallon**)
              Bucket, small basket containing pair of drawers, snuff-box
                  (**Granny Trill**)
              Kindling (**Boys**)
              Coffin on cart (**Actor**)
              Giant cloth (**Cast**)
              Sketching book (**Tony**)
              Basket (**Doth** or **Phyll**)
              Song sheet (**Vicar**)
              Practical lanterns (**Children**)
              Cart with large flagon of cider (**Cast**)
              Posy of wild roses (**Mother**)

Personal: **Granny Trill**: spectacles in apron pocket
              Squire: pince-nez

LIGHTING PLOT

ACT I

To open: House Lights down

Cue 1	**Solo voice:** "Laid over my eyes ..." *Bring up full lighting*	(Page 1)
Cue 2	**Laurie:** "... many times like a snowstorm toy ..." *Reduce lighting to interior evening effect*	(Page 2)
Cue 3	**Laurie:** "It was for me alone ... " *Gradually bring up shaft of light through the screen*	(Page 3)
Cue 4	**Mother** exits *Continue to increase lighting until it comes up to full*	(Page 3)
Cue 5	**Chorus:** " Miss, can I go?" *Change to overhead lighting to give silhouette effect*	(Page 10)
Cue 6	**Laurie:** "Many a lone ..." *Crossfade to spot on* **Laurie**	(Page 11)
Cue 7	The children enter and set up the table *Crossfade to warm interior effect on c area with darkness beyond*	(Page 11)
Cue 8	**Jack** mimes lighting the lamp *Bring up covering spot for lamp and increase lighting overall*	(Page 12)
Cue 9	**Doth** turns out the lamp *Snap off covering spot and reduce lighting*	(Page 15)
Cue 10	**Laurie:** "... clawed the dark curtains back." *Harsh moonlight effect on group*	(Page 16)
Cue 11	**Marge** mimes relighting the lamp *Change to warm interior effect*	(Page 16)

Cue 12	**Marge**: "... are the limit!" *Change to cold winter effect*	(Page 21)
Cue 13	**Mother**: "Haunting night and day." *Fade lighting on boys in bed*	(Page 23)
Cue 14	The **girls** and **Mother** exit *Star effect behind gauze screen; moonlight effect overall*	(Page 24)
Cue 15	**Laurie**: "A boy, time fixed in ice ..." *Snow effect*	(Page 24)
Cue 16	**Laurie**: "Locked in this paradise." *·Slow fade to black-out*	(Page 25)

ACT II

To open: Very dim lighting

Cue 17	Thunder *Lightning*	(Page 26)
Cue 18	**Mother**: "... things to put up with." *Lightning*	(Page 26)
Cue 19	**Laurie**: " ... through rain in peace." *Bring up general lighting*	(Page 27)
Cue 20	**Laurie**: "... every corner of the house." *Colour effect on screens*	(Page 27)
Cue 21	**Laurie**: "... Granny Trill had none of them." *Change to green mottled light*	(Page 28)
Cue 22	**Laurie**: "... then for ever." *Crossfade to spot behind **Granny Trill***	(Page 30)
Cue 23	**Trill**: "I dunno." *Crossfade to spot behind **Granny Wallon***	(Page 30)
Cue 24	**Wallon**: "You mark my words." *Crossfade to woodland effect*	(Page 30)

EFFECTS PLOT

ACT I

ACT II

Cue 12   **Mother**: " ... the house straight."   (Page 26)
            Thunder

Cue 13   **Laurie**: " ... into every corner of the house."   (Page 27)
            White flowers projection on circular area

Cue 14   **Laurie**: "The little church ——"   (Page 31)
            Bell tolls

Cue 15   **Laurie**: " ... than anyone else."   (Page 31)
            Wind

Cue 16   **Mrs Davies**: " Come on up, then."   (Page 32)
            Wind

Cue 17   The **Barmaid** enters   (Page 32)
            Wind howls; continue

Cue 18   **Laurie**: " ... against the storm."   (Page 33)
            Wind stops

Cue 19   **Mother**: "' ... and *that* was long before Adam!'" (Page 37)
            Sound of pony and trap

Cue 20   The cast sit astride chairs in a circle   (Page 40)
            Hurdy-gurdy music

Cue 21   The **Narrator** collects the fares   (Page 40)
            Cut hurdy-gurdy music; sound of incoming tide

Cue 22   **Laurie**: "When the tide went out ..."   (Page 41)
            Cut sound of incoming tide

Cue 23   **Laurie**: "And the Outing was over!"   (Page 41)
            Tinkly piano music

Cue 24   The carol singers exit   (Page 45)
            Birdsong

Cue 25   Everyone exits   (Page 46)
            Birdsong

Act II
59

Cue 26   **Rosie** vanishes   (Page 48)
           Owl cries

Cue 27   **Laurie**: *"Yes,* and *back again!"*   (Page 48)
           Owl hoots

Cue 28   **Laurie**: " ... the last days of the village."   (Page 49)
           Dance music played on piano

CPSIA information can be obtained
at www.ICGtesting.com
Printed in the USA
BVHW030915010922
645933BV00005B/540